Time's Now/Ya es Tiempo

by/por
Miguel Algarín

Arte Público Press
Houston, Texas
1985

This publication is made possible through a grant from
The National Endowment for the Arts, a federal agency.

Cover design by Narciso Peña
Cover art and center illustration by D. McNair

Books by Miguel Algarín:

Mongo Affair, 1978.
On Call, 1980.
Body Bee Calling from the 21st Century, 1982.
Song of Protest, by Pablo Neruda
(translated by Miguel Algarín), 1975.
Nuyorican Poetry
(edited by Miguel Algarín and Miguel Piñero), 1975.

Arte Público Press
University of Houston
University Park
Houston, Texas 77004

Library of Congress Catalog No. 83-072575
ISBN 0-934770-336
Copyright © 1985 Miguel Algarín
Printed in the United States of America

CONTENTS/CONTENIDO

III. Conversations with Silence/
Conversaciones con el Silencio

Para Puerto Rico en memoria de
Miguel Adolfo Fitte Loperena
Lobo

On Time's Now

It was a mild, October afternoon in Manhattan, the streets of little Italy were teeming with people. We ate lunch at Luna's, Miguel's favorite place, then we walked up Canal Street to the Manhattan Bridge, then turned down the Bowery toward the Lower East Side. Miguel was giving me a tour through his streets, his turf. He took the time to pause, to show things to me, so I could see his world as he sees it.

Yo veo,
tú ves,
y cuando yo veo lo que tú ves,
el espacio entre tú y yo desaparece . . .

Miguel Algarín is consumed by his world, and the consummation is an infectious love he passes on to all he meets. He is a city poet, a city shaman whose "conversations with silence" lead us to the truth. For Miguel, love is the truth.

A long afternoon later, and we paused at MacSorley's to drink ale. That's where Miguel read his *Time's Now* en español. He read with an intensity of emotion which characterizes Miguel the man, un amor that filled the bar and drew the people together, to listen to his lyrical Españoloriquen, the language of his madre isla.

Daily dealings, that's the name of the first section of poems, and Miguel knows la brega diaria of his Manhattan universe. Daily dealings is life, and for the poet life is meaningful if there is love and art. Love and art can unite time, the past, present and future. And in that space of time there's creation, the creation of Nuyorican art to which Miguel and his fellow artists are devoted. There in the Lower East Side at the Nuyorican Poets Cafe they're creating the center of a new universe; there they have given birth to la canción de los Nuyoricans, los Puertorriqueños de la nueva isla, Manhattan.

Puerto Rico es la madre, Manhattan is the new father, a harsher, crueler father at times, at times a generous father. Miguel Algarín is a man who straddles the islands, he connects, he builds his bridge there on the Loisaida of Manhattan, and now the world is coming to hear the songs and see the theatre of the Nuyorican Poets Cafe.

The poems moved me, immediately. I write these notes as my response, because Miguel understood that the poem goes out to connect, to share, and if I as a Chicano from the Rio Grande could make the connection to his world, then he had built one more bridge, and now the isla of Manhattan was connected to the isla of Aztlán.

My impressions of the day, the poems, the poet. A simple man with an infectious, elfish grin, a scholar, a man of the world who has trudged across the frozen waste of Siberia to still the senses, a sensuous man who has been enraptured in the delight of senses on a boat trip up the virgin Amazon. A contradiction, no, a complex man, yes. He knew that between Siberia and the Amazon there lay a space he needed to connect, and so he went. He is obsessed with the duality in the cosmos, with the frightening space in the soul.

The chemistry Miguel seeks is in his senses which drives Miguel's poetry. If Manhattan is power, the power can create reality or illusion. Miguel senses the center of that power in the media, the good and bad of radio, news, television. In the wrong hands, the media can drive fear into the heart.

they rape us with Cable T.V. — the invisible spy — transmitting while appearing to be off.

The cure cures us with procuring,
you're procured, I'm procured
they procure us with the cure . . .

In part two, the hard, political reality enters the space of the poet. The poems lose some of their lyricism. Media and political statement are aimed at the gut. If Manhattan is threatened, then the entire world is threatened, for the poet Manhattan is the microcosm.

"There is a song of nations in my heart," says Miguel with the gusto and emotional intensity of a Whitman. Like Whitman, Miguel is concerned with the creation of a new space on the American mainland, the space of his Caribbean world mixed with the daily dealings of the American hustle. And the only hope is love, the love suckled from la madre isla, no matter how many generations ago. History lives in the soul of the poet.

"Yo soy el tiempo," he says in one of his songs. Yo soy. He affirms the "aquí estoy" position of the Puertorriqueño. The affirmation of the poet is a new power, a new kind of power found in the silence of his religious conversations. The poet can create space and in that space man and woman can recreate themselves. Es la magia del poeta, el shaman de la isla.

Not all the media is negative. Some teaches, some brings the music, the rhythm of syllables, the beat which works its way into his poetry. The image of the mother appears, she who sang songs of illusion in the kitchen, she who taught the poet. Radio music fills the air. Listen to the beat, the mother sang, the radio played, every single syllable counts, down to the last period. This is a poet who makes every single syllable count, because every beat on the street, on the radio, in life, counts, as every second counts.

9

There is space in the poetry. The poem creates space, as it creates the intensity of coming together. Between Manhattan and Puerto Rico there is space, and love can fill that space. Silence is space. The paradox is that at the moment of unity more space is created, but now it is the boundless space of love. This is the emotion I feel in the poems, that endless space of love. In that space, all the islands come together: man the island, woman the island, Manhattan, Puerto Rico, Aztlán, Cuba, El Salvador, Nicaragua, and on and on.

The only caution is not to miss a single syllable, because to miss the beat is to miss the point through which you enter the boundless space, and if you don't enter the space of love, you can't open yourself up to daily dealings and communication and the silence of love.

Rudolfo A. Anaya
Isla de Aztlán
New Mexico

I

Daily dealings in South, Central and North America
La brega diaria en el Sur, Centro y Norte de las Américas

Relish

I'm frightened by so much heat,
sweating so much desire, sliding,
greased by tenderness,
enduring the sensual whirlpool
of your lips moistened by mutual saliva,
your hands caressing
my juices, transforming them into flesh,
made of blood and sperm,
the only actual possibility
for desire become the gelatin
of you and me
writhing in the sea.

Sabrosura

Me da miedo sentir tanto calor,
sudar tanto deseo, resbalar,
engrasado por la ternura,
que perdura en el remolino sensual
de tus labios mojados con saliva mutua,
tus manos acariciando
mi sabrosura, convirtiéndola en carne,
construida de sangre y leche,
la única posibilidad actual,
del deseo hecho el tembleque
de tú y yo
estrujándonos en el mar.

Life

What could be said about her?
except she's a hole,
and to be happy is to occupy that space,
since the world is for me,
not for anybody,
since there aren't any sincere folks,
even though those who comply exist,
carrying a harvest of brotherliness,
that consumes them
in a short life
where love is evil,
and warmth, the timid sweet
of an overwhelming bitterness.

La vida

¿Qué se podría decir de ella?
sino que es un roto,
y el estar alegre es el ocupar ese espacio,
ya que el mundo es para uno,
no para nadie,
ya que de los sinceros no hay,
aunque cumplidores se encuentran,
cargando su cosecha de hermandad,
que los consume
en una vida corta,
donde el amor es la maldad,
y el cariño, el tímido dulce
de una agridez total.

Fighting

"What do you want,
that we be looked at?
Well, they've seen us!
But, so that you know,
I'm here because I love you,"
that's what she says,
suspecting the intentions
of the man who's kissing her,
"though that's enough! Let's forget it," she continues,
"because I've stopped running from you."

Peleando

"¿Qué tú quieres,
que nos vean?
¡Pues, nos vieron!
pero, para que lo sepas,
yo estoy aquí porque te quiero,"
así dice ella,
sospechando la intención
de él que la besa,
"¡aunque basta! Olvidémoslo," sigue ella,
"porque yo ya dejé de huirte."

But with a difference

Change arrives,
a new medicinal rhythm pulverizes pain,
I search the flow of a song
that surges for you, for me,
sweet melody that screams:
what's for me?
with change there's difference,
showing steps not taken,
offering kisses that begin to fill,
lips that start to nourish,
tongue that washes,
hands that relieve,
arms that embrace change without fear.

Pero con la diferencia

Llega el cambio,
y un nuevo ritmo medicinal pulveriza el dolor.
Busco la fuente de una canción
que surge para ti, para mí,
dulce melodía que grita:
"¿y para mí qué?"
Con el cambio llega la diferencia,
enseñándome pasos no dados,
ofreciendo besos que empiezan a llenar,
labios que llegan a nutrir,
lengua que lava,
manos que alivian,
brazos que abrazan el cambio sin miedo.

In an encounter

The signals
are localized
then
the thorns are boiled
in miraculous evil
where roses burn
the body is stone
the light clean, fleeting
the shadow walks
open to the wind
waiting to be loved.

En un encuentro

Se localizan
las señales
después
se hierven las espinas
en la maldad maravillosa
donde las rosas arden
el cuerpo es de piedra
la luz limpia, fugaz
la sombra camina
abierta al viento
esperando ser amada.

We

I'll let it go
I'll stop running from you
Now I look to find you
at the eye's center
where you reflect
that I am time
and you the hour of two beings
that approach.

Nosotros

Ya lo dejo
Dejaré de alejarme
Ahora busco encontrarte
en el propio centro del ojo
donde tú reflejas
que yo soy el tiempo
y tú la hora de dos seres
que se aproximan.

My proposal is that . . .

I want to live with you,
enjoy first, then procreate
children for the new century,
leaving clues and roots,
a nettling that repels,
and receives what was,
converting it into what is,
I want to unite bodies,
sowing space
for two tying a knot.

Mi propuesta es que . . .

Me gustaría vivir contigo,
gozar primero, después procrear
criaturas para el nuevo siglo,
dejando huellas y raíces,
inquietudes que rechazan
y reciben lo que fue,
convirtiéndolo en lo que es.
Me gustaría unir cuerpos,
sembrando espacio
para dos atar un nudo.

Right to the grain

When we look at each other,
our hearts shudder,
so that when we speak it hurts,
but we've only talked about a few things.
Now we're approaching
the sweet and turbulent tenderness of loving.

Yendo al grano

Cuando nos miramos,
se nos estremece el corazón.
Así que el hablarnos duele,
pero sólo nos hemos dicho unas tres cosas.
Ahora nos arrimamos
a la dulce y turbulenta ternura del amar.

Where

I have a small fence
that surrounds my fair home
where I propose and propound
where I invent and discover.
What's this responding
this having to signal where I am
what I want
and what I see?
How much responsibility do I owe the blue/yellow
that attracts my eye
at your entering my home,
fair dwelling where the years drown?

Donde

Tengo una verjita,
que rodea mi lindo hogar,
donde propongo y pongo,
donde invento y encuentro,
¿Qué es este responder,
este tener que señalar dónde estoy?
¿Qué deseo,
y qué es lo que veo?
¿Cuánta responsabilidad le debo al azul/amarillo
que atrae mi ojo
al tú entrar en mi casita,
lindo hogar donde los años se ahogan?

Day after day

What there is repeats
     WA
     LK
     ING
over everything that comes
towards an eye that absorbs
red words excusing
the green error over which the burning
early morning yellow sun triumphs
into the white heat of mid-day
that mixes into a red afternoon
conceding to the dark black nightfall.

Día tras día

Se repite lo que hay
     CA
     MI
     NA
sobre todo lo que viene
hacia un ojo que recoge
palabras rojas disculpando
el error verde que deja triunfar al amarillo
sol del amanecer quemando hasta convertirse
en el fuego blanco del mediodía
que se transforma en un rojo atardecer
vencido por el negro oscuro del anochecer.

And to play it back

I love you more than the yesterday and today of our being,
I embrace you wanting more
of what was
of what we have
and of what there will be.
Today, on your birthday, I wish you what there is.

Y vuelve

Yo te quiero más que el ayer y el hoy de nuestro ser,
te abrazo deseando más
de lo que hubo
de lo que tenemos
y de lo que habrá.
Hoy, en tu feliz santo, te deseo lo que hay.

Dealing with . . .

The end is a fair step forward
and what's worked out
between that step and the past
is what folks used to call the present.

Bregando con . . .

El final es un lindo paso al frente
y lo que se brega
entre ese paso y el pasado
es lo que la gente llamaba el presente.

Although love in reverse

It's not that it spills,
but that it hits, bites,
burns, breaks, destroys
what in righteousness gets done.
In discord love negates,
the chair bludgeons the scalp,
blood flows and dries
the motives of a warring love.

Aunque el amor al revés

No es que se pierde,
sino que pega, muerde,
quema, quiebra, destruye
lo que al derecho se ha hecho.
Al revés el cariño niega,
la silla atropella el cabello,
la sangre brota y reseca
el intento de un amor guerrero.

On Eleventh Street, Barrio Obrero
(September 11, 1941)

I am a place,
against which
life can rebel,
an entire Nation can wage war against it,
without knowing that what is,
comes from what gets done,
by an I bearing contrariness
looking for specific light.

En la Calle Once, Barrio Obrero
(Septiembre 11, 1941)

El yo es un punto,
contra el cual la vida
se puede rebelar.
Una nación entera le puede declarar guerra
sin entender que lo que es,
será lo que se ha hecho
por un yo que lleva la contrariedad
buscando cierta claridad.

In Santurce's Light

I choose to move without stopping,
always on the lookout
for the step taken as print
of an immediate past that seeps,
dripping, entering into
where the moment plays.
I am sweating in a here
made of what I did yesterday,
that today is the what's to be of what I do now.
Check it out! Look at how this being breathes.

En la luz de Santurce

Elijo moverme sin parar
y no dejo de mirar
el paso ya dado como huella
de un pasado inmediato que se escurre,
goteándose, entrando la presencia actual,
donde el momento se desenlaza.
Me encuentro sudando en un aquí
labrado en lo que hice ayer,
que hoy es lo que será de lo que ahora hago,
¡fíjate! mira como respira este ser.

At the Electronic Frontier

I search the chemistry of specific emotions,
a combination of earth and air
that evokes the vital detail,
the phrase that heats the frying pan,
the look that smiles,
offering signals that localize,
where I am, and clarify what I see.
I'm child of the Electronic Frontier.
I learn off the radio waves
of 98.7 Kiss F.M. salsa/disco jams,
that come from a Sony,
bought even though I need a coat,
even though I'm behind on my payments
for the Trinitron Remote Control Color T.V.
that I picked up at Crazy Eddie's last month.
I'm child of the Columbia Space Shuttle,
and I need to know all the electronic gimmicks
invented yesterday
that are already primitive cousins
to those developed today
from eight to five P.M. in Japan.

En la Frontera Electrónica

Busco la química de cierta emoción,
combinación de tierra y aire
que saca el detalle útil,
la frase que le da fuego al sartén,
la mirada que sonríe,
ofreciendo señales que localizan
dónde estoy y aclaran lo que veo.
Soy hijo de la Frontera Electrónica,
me educo en las ondas radiales
de la 98.7 Kiss F.M. salsa/disco jams
que salen de un radio Sony
comprado a pesar de que necesito abrigo,
a pesar de que me atraso con los pagos a plazo
del televisor a control remoto, Trinitron a colores
que compré el mes pasado en Crazy Eddie.
Soy hijo del Columbia Space Shuttle
y necesito conocer los embelecos electrónicos
inventados ayer
que ya son los primos primitivos
de los que se desarrollaron hoy
desde las ocho hasta las cinco de la tarde en el Japón.

II

Newspapers
(radio and television)

Periódicos
(la radio y la televisión)

Fear

They hear us, see us, they pursue us
into toilets, classrooms, stores
they spy on us pissing between parked cars
they peep every signal transmitted
they envy our private meditations
they wring every pure emotion out of us
born of our trust
they rape us with Cable T.V. — the invisible spy —
transmitting while appearing to be off.
The cure cures us with procuring,
you're procured, I'm procured,
they procure us with the cure,
curing us in the midst of a battle
that destroys before the cure cures this pure lunacy.

Miedo

Ellos nos oyen, nos ven, nos persiguen
a los inodoros, a los salones, a las tiendas
nos notan toda señal transmitida
nos añoran nuestras meditaciones privadas
nos escurren cada gota de emoción pura
inspirada en nuestra confianza
nos violan con el espía invisible de la televisión por cable
que transmite cuando el ojo aparenta dormir.
La cura nos cura con la procura.
Te procuran, me procuran,
nos procuran con la cura,
curándonos en medio de una batalla
que destruye antes de que la cura cure esta pura locura.

Though there's a new prayer: first part
(to three cowboys)

A new trinity arrives
in the name of Father Reagan,
of the Holy Spirit Haig
and the Son Weinberger, amen.
Tonight there's a religious act:
the meaning, eternal moment,
where the hillbillie leaves for the city,
dancing on down the road
to buy for his Mom's at the jewelers
the pearl of the seas, slave Borinquen,
free for six months, possessed for four hundred years,
giving it to his old lady,
who visualizes the Space Shuttle
taking and bringing the powerful,
leaving my parents in Queens,
where they die and live,
where my mother invents a thousand melodies
for the mid-day, light-orange
and pale, full of spume
that roll up on the mortal
sands of a city that sweats knives
of competition
between the Lord and his eternal Servant.
Already it's seen that the trinity ferments,
that lies dominate,
that the Japanese pay Allen off,
that Reagan equivocates,
that he splits into thirty pieces at once,
crucifying global trust,
that's how the divine trinity falters.

Aunque hay una nueva oración: primera parte
(a tres vaqueros)

Ha llegado una nueva trinidad,
en el nombre del Padre Reagan,
del Espíritu Haig
y del hijo Weinberger, amén.
Esta noche se celebra un acto sacramental,
el significado, eterno momento,
donde el jibarito sale para la ciudad,
bailando así por el camino,
hacia la joyería a comprarle a su madre
la perla de los mares, la esclava Borinquen,
libre por seis meses, poseída por cuatrocientos años,
regalándosela a su viejita,
la cual visualiza el Space Shuttle
saliendo y llevando a los poderosos,
dejando a mis padres en Queens
donde se mueren y viven,
donde mi madre se inventa miles de melodías
para el mediodía, anaranjadas
y pálidas, llenas de espumas
que se desbordan en la arena
mortal de una ciudad que suda cuchillas
de la competencia
entre el Señor y su eterno Servidor.
Ya se ve que la trinidad fomenta,
que la mentira domina,
que los japoneses le pagan a Allen,
que Reagan ya miente,
que revienta en treinta pedazos a la vez,
crucificando la confianza mundial,
así ya falla la divina trinidad.

Look at the first lesson: second part
(the newspapers)

The Secretary of State Alexander Haig,
disturbed by Washington's gossip,
telephoned Jack Anderson attacking
certain White House aides
as guerrillas bombarding
the matrimony of trust between him and Mr. Reagan.
It's said Mr. Haig found himself
so perturbed
so hurt
so nettled
that the Secretary of State
made a late night phone call to Mr. Anderson
assuring him anxiously
of the firm, constant friendship
and confidence he enjoys with Mr. Reagan:
"No one will weaken it."
But meanwhile,
our cowboy, our Haig,
stirring up a vigorous campaign
dares to call his Chief Reagan
asking a thousand pardons for the bother
but giving orders to the Chief
to break his peace and rest in Camp David
and call Jack Anderson so that
the mortal lie
not reach the press,
that he is no longer wanted in the White House
and that they have him on a disappointment list
with a foot on a banana peel.

Fíjense en la primera lección: segunda parte
(los periódicos)

El Secretario de Estado Alexander Haig,
molesto por los bochinches de Washington,
telefoneó a Jack Anderson atacando a
ciertos Ayudantes de la Casa Blanca
como guerrilleros bombardeando
el matrimonio de confianza entre él y el Sr. Reagan.
Se dice que el Sr. Haig se encontró
tan perturbado
tan herido
tan pullado
que el Secretario de Estado
hizo una llamada telefónica tarde en la noche
    al Sr. Anderson
ansiosamente asegurándole
la firme y constante amistad
y confianza que él goza con el Sr. Reagan:
"nadie la afligirá,"
pero mientras tanto,
nuestro vaquero, nuestro Haig,
formando una campaña vigorosa,
se atreve a llamar a su Jefe Reagan
pidiéndole mil excusas por la molestia
pero dándole órdenes al Jefe
que rompa su paz y descanso en Camp David
y llame a Jack Anderson, cosa de que
el embuste mortal
no salga a la prensa,
que a él ya no lo quieren en la Casa Blanca
y que lo tienen en la lista de los desnombrados,
con un pie sobre una cáscara de guineo.

While Morazán is on the evening news: first part

El Salvador asphyxiates
while I'm into an infinite gaze
at the sprouting quarrel,
participating in events that by afternoon
become the content of the 7 o'clock news.
Today El Salvador occupies space
on the twelfth page of the *New York Post*.
There's a photo of Two Salvadorans
shooting at each other
because the fog created by Washington
blinds them, El Salvador burns,
the guerrillas have taken Morazán,
Haig doesn't know who to hug.
Should he give a hand to the guerrilla who's winning
or the military forces that are losing?
But the struggle changes every second.
Who to love is the White House dilemma
while El Salvador explodes.

Mientras Morazán se encuentra en las noticias de la tarde: primera parte

El Salvador se asfixia
mientras me encuentro viendo infinitamente
la riña en desarrollo,
participando en eventos que al atardecer
ya son el contenido de las Noticias de las Siete.
Hoy El Salvador ocupa espacio
en la página doce del *New York Post*.
Hay una foto de dos salvadoreños
disparando uno contra el otro
porque la tiniebla creada en Washington
los ciega, El Salvador quema,
los guerrilleros se apoderan de Morazán,
Haig ya no sabe a quién abrazar,
si darle la mano al guerrillero que ganando va
o al ejército que perdiendo está,
pero al segundo la batalla cambia.
A quién querer es el dilema de la Casa Blanca
mientras El Salvador explota.

Elections and . . .: second part

"People go out to vote
but the guerrillas obstruct them."
That's what's said on Channel 4 in Manhattan.
On the 28th of March we're made to understand
that Democracy is being obstructed
by the left, "the guerrillas
fire against the Salvadoran people,"
but that chaos was invented in the White House
and it doesn't afflict the public in Chatatenango,
there aren't any guarantees
for the public to take hold of!
although some go out and vote pretending
that the machinery is not fraudulent,
that Duarte doesn't repress,
not withstanding that it's written in every man's bible,
that in El Salvador Christ has not yet
freed his folk.

Elecciones y . . .: segunda parte

"La gente sale a votar
y los guerrilleros impiden,"
así se dice en el Canal 4 en Manhattan.
Nos dan a entender el 28 de marzo
que la Democracia está obstruida
por la izquierda, "el guerrillero
dispara contra el pueblo salvadoreño,"
pero ese caos fue inventado en la Casa Blanca
y no aflige al público de Chatatenango.
¡No hay garantías!
para que el pueblo se entregue
aunque algunos salen a votar fingiendo
que no hay fraude en el proceso,
que Duarte no oprime,
no obstante, se lee en el evangelio cotidiano
que el Cristo Salvadoreño no ha logrado
liberar a su pueblo.

A defiance

England and Argentina are spoused,
tied by the long Atlantic rope.
Today the wives are hand-cuffed,
fighting and bombarding the Falklands,
looking for right of possession.
"The Falklands are mine,"
says Margaret.
"No, their ours,"
says Nicanor.
What shame!
So many die,
Latin America betrayed,
England protected,
backed up by the United States!
Thus in the extreme blue of the South Atlantic,
there're two dolls handcuffed,
fighting, sprouting a global quarrel.

Un desafío

Inglaterra y la Argentina son esposas,
atadas por la larga soga del Atlántico.
Hoy las esposas esposadas
se pelean y bombardean Las Malvinas
buscando datos de posesión,
"Las Malvinas son nuestras,"
dice Margaret.
"No, son nuestras,"
dice Nicanor.
¡Qué pena!
matan a tantos,
Latinoamérica traicionada,
Inglaterra apoyada,
¡respaldada por los estadounidenses!
así en el extremo azul del Sur Atlántico
se encuentran dos muñecas esposadas,
batallándose, creando una riña mundial.

And it's said that meanwhile . . .

Mr. Haig implores England
not to humiliate Argentina,
to win and straighten out the quarrel
that disturbs and debilitates the tie
among all the other slaves
of the Organization of American States.
England wins,
Argentina loses.
That's what the press/television tells us in New York.
But
what do Argentinians know?
What do we know here?
Who knows what should be known?
Does truth have a point
where life's reality begins its eternal parade
or is truth
the golden dream of lies?

Y se dice que mientras tanto . . .

El Señor Haig le implora a la Inglaterra
no humille a la Argentina,
que gane y calle la riña
que ya molesta y debilita el lazo
con todos los otros esclavos
de la Organización de Estados Americanos.
Inglaterra gana,
la Argentina pierde.
Así nos dice la prensa/televisión en Nueva York.
¿Pero?
¿Qué sabrá el pueblo argentino?
¿Qué sabemos nosotros aquí?
¿Quién sabe lo que hay que saber?
¿Tiene la verdad un punto
donde principia el eterno desfile de la realidad
o es la verdad
el sueño dorado de la mentira?

Look at Nicaragua

Jeanne Kirkpatrick says:
"Nicaragua lives in fear,"
but Nuyoricans know more than that.

Miren a Nicaragua

Jeanne Kirkpatrick dice:
"Nicaragua vive en miedo,"
pero el Nuyorican sabe más que eso.

And in the U.S.A.
(State of emergency in New Brunswick, N.J.)

If something is not done
Criminal Justice will collapse,
or worse, there will be riots in jails
just like those in Essex, Union and Bergen Counties.
Prisons overflow, they can't hold,
there's no space, the courts dismiss everything,
only extreme cases are retained,
though it's still difficult to hold on to
people who react with brutal crimes.
The hitch is in the rapid dismissals,
can't keep up with those handcuffed,
the courts are jammed,
the list of fugitives grows.
If beds aren't found,
the jails'll explode,
set on fire by inmates
who yield to violent passions.

Y en los E.E.U.U.
(Emergencia en New Brunswick, N.J.)

Si no se hace algo inmediatamente,
se desplomará la justicia criminal
o, peor, habrá motines en las cárceles
tal como ha pasado en los condados de Essex,
    Union y Bergen.
Las prisiones se desbordan, no aguantan,
no hay espacio, las cortes despiden todo.
Sólo se quedan con casos extremos
y aún se hace difícil retener
a los que reaccionan con crímenes brutales.
El truco es la rapidez del despacho.
No alcanza a los que esposan,
las cortes se inundan,
la lista de fugitivos se alarga,
si no se encuentran camas
las cárceles explotarán,
incendiadas por los encarcelados,
por los que a la pasión violenta se entregan.

But Jacobo Timmerman knows . . .

that Argentina's fighting
the first battles
of the Third World War while
I seek to procure in New York
a direct phone line to Buenos Aires
to know! what to do?
when the quarrel sprouts
and comes close without my seeing it,
although Arabs already peddle in Manhattan
and the Japanese pin Hawaii on themselves
like a tiny electronic candy-bar
jewel in the Pacific,
giving them credit-plans into New York.

Pero Jacobo Timmerman sabe . . .

que en la Argentina pelean
las primaras batallas
de la Tercera Guerra Mundial mientras
yo busco en Nueva York procurarme
una línea telefónica a Buenos Aires
¡para así saber! ¿qué hacer?
cuando el desarreglo se desarrolle
y se acerque sin yo verlo,
aunque ya los árabes venden en Manhattan
y los japoneses se prenden a Hawaii
como un bomboncito electrónico,
una joya en el Pacífico,
dándoles pagos a plazo hacia Nueva York.

Even though . . .

Menachem Begin solicits,
and Yasser Arafat mortifies
the biblical peace never found
in an instance never realized,
what can be said when losing?
at not wanting to surrender!
Arafat's trapped, encircled,
and should he count on Ronald Reagan
to break loose with thunder
against Israel, he'll see how frail
this human stay is,
because "Nobody is
        going to
        bring Israel
        to her knees
        . . . Jews
        do not kneel
        but to God."

Aunque ya . . .

Menachem Begin solicita,
y Yasser Arafat mortifica
la paz bíblica nunca encontrada
en un momento no hecho,
¿qué se dice al perder?
¡al no querer rendirse!
Arafat está atrapado, enredado,
y si cuenta con Ronald Reagan
para que rompa a relámpagos
contra Israel, verá lo mortal
de esta temporada humana,
porque "nadie arrodillará
      a Israel.
      . . . Los judíos
      no se arrodillan
      sino a Dios."

III

Conversations with Silence

Conversaciones con el Silencio

Conversation number one with the Holy Spirit

I write
to a listener
whose chemistry
is changed
on hearing these words.

Conversación número uno con el Espíritu Santo

Yo le escribo
a un oyente
cuya química
queda cambiada
al oír estas palabras.

Conversation number two with Jesus

The I, is, a verb,
the verb, is, an action,
with the verb a mystery begins,
with the movement of words
emotion is contained,
the magic is to run
through the tongue's veins
what you intend to speak,
make happen.

Conversación número dos con Jesús

El yo, es, un verbo,
el verbo, es, la acción,
con el verbo empieza el misterio,
con el movimiento de palabras
se contiene la emoción,
la magia es correr
por las venas de la lengua,
lo que se intenta hablar,
hacer pasar.

Conversation number three with the Father, the Son and the Holy Spirit

I
The soul is joy
and the heart love
because nobody wants to suffer.

II
The soul is sadness
and the heart pain
because nobody can avoid it.

III
I go
alone
hoping you understand
that it is so
because I choose it.

Conversación número tres con el Padre, el Hijo y el Espíritu Santo

I
El alma es alegría
y el corazón amor
porque sufrir nadie quiere.

II
El alma es pena
y el corazón dolor
porque evitarlo nadie puede.

III
Me voy
sólo
esperando entiendan
que así es
porque así lo quiero.

Conversation number four with the Holy Trinity

I would like to fill your being,
but if I refuse,
it isn't that I reject your beauty,
it's that it's impossible
to share my I with your you.

Conversación número cuatro con la Santa Trinidad

Me gustaría llenar tu ser,
pero si lo rechazo,
no es que desprecio tu belleza,
sino que se me hace imposible
compartir mi yo con tu tú.

Conversation number five with Christ

I see,
you see,
and when I see what you see,
the space between you and I disappears,
but I still despair,
because I don't know if you've done what I did,
in order to see what you see.

Conversación número cinco con Cristo

Yo veo,
tú ves,
y cuando yo veo lo que tú ves,
el espacio entre tú y yo desaparece,
pero todavía desespero,
porque no sé si tú hiciste lo que yo hice,
para lograr ver lo que tú ves.

Conversation number six with Our Lord

When I am at ease
with my *I am* in front of your *you are*,
trust melts my fear,
I begin to love you
with no dread of losing myself in a *we are*
where we share, keeping no secrets.

Conversación número seis con Nuestro Señor

Cuando me siento cómodo
con mi *yo soy* frente a tu *tú eres*,
la confianza derrite mi miedo,
empiezo a quererte
sin temer perderme en un *nosotros*
donde compartimos sin guardar secretos.